I'M SO FREAKING
FREAKED OUT

Created, published, and distributed by Knock Knock
6080 Center Drive
Los Angeles, CA 90045
knockknockstuff.com
Knock Knock is a registered trademark of Knock Knock LLC
Inner-Truth is a registered trademark of Knock Knock LLC

This book is meant solely for entertainment purposes. In no event will
Knock Knock be liable to any reader for any harm, injury, or damages,
including direct, indirect, incidental, special, consequential, or punitive
arising out of or in connection with the use of the information contained
in this book. So there.

ISBN: 978-160106760-9
UPC: 825703-50082-0

YOU'RE SO FREAKING
FREAKED
OUT! OF COURSE YOU ARE.

Wars, epidemics, recessions, homelessness, climate change, bad grammar, the end of Saturday morning cartoons: it's a wonder we all haven't lost our minds. How do you deal?

How do you get through the day without curling up into a ball at the slightest provocation? How do you keep your brain from churning in the middle of the night, when even the most benign things can seem overwhelming? (OH GOD. I HAVE NO CLEAN SOCKS. IS THAT AN OWL IN THE CORNER OF THE ROOM?)

You're in good company. Even though we know there are many ways to manage anxiety, from pharmaceuticals to meditation to vacations in Belize, everyone loses it sometimes. And if you read one of the zillion how-to articles on relaxation and dealing with stress, you'll learn that one of the handiest and most cost-effective ways to channel your freak-outs is to write them down.

Researchers have shown in a variety of ways how writing about fears can help alleviate them. For instance, psychologists at the University of Chicago learned that if students wrote down their feelings ten minutes before an exam, they improved their performance. According to *UChicago News*, "The writing exercise allowed students to unload their anxieties before taking the test and accordingly freed up brainpower needed to complete the test successfully—brainpower that is normally occupied by worries about the test."

Journal writing also facilitates another doctor-recommended way to ease stress—creating a designated "worry time." *LiveScience*, reporting on research from the Netherlands, notes that it actually works to postpone panic, so that it doesn't take over every minute of the day. "By compartmentalizing worry—setting aside a specific half-hour period each day to think about worries and consider solutions, and also deliberately avoiding thinking about those issues the rest of the day—people can ultimately help reduce those worries, research has shown."

A journal—besides being a place to unload concerns, trivial or not—has been shown to have other powerful benefits. As noted self-help guru Deepak Chopra claims, "Journaling is one of the most powerful tools we have to transform our lives," and there is consistent evidence that journal writing aids physical health. According to a widely cited study by James W. Pennebaker and Janel D. Seagal, "Writing about important personal experiences in an emotional way... brings about improvements in mental and physical health." Proven benefits include better stress management (woot!), strengthened immune systems, fewer doctor visits, and improvement in chronic illnesses such as asthma.

It's not entirely clear how journaling accomplishes all this. Catharsis is involved, but many also point to the value of organizing experiences into a cohesive narrative. According to *Newsweek*, some experts believe that journaling "forces us to transform the ruminations cluttering our minds into coherent stories." You can't argue with the professionals: write about your fears and they won't be so big and scary.

Clearly, you're no stranger to a journal's value, or you wouldn't be reading this now. But how should you use it? Specialists agree that in order to reap the benefits of journaling you have to stick with it, quasi-daily, for as little as five minutes at a time (at least fifteen minutes, however, is best). Call it your designated worry time. Finding regular writing times and comfortable locations can help with consistency.

Write about what's stressing you out and what scares you, no matter how overwhelming or preposterous. Is it the meeting tomorrow or a conflict with your oldest friend? Are you nervous that you'll blow the test or that your project sucks? Are you afraid that Dracula is hiding in your bathroom or that you will get some yet-to-be-discovered fatal illness? Imagine the worst-case scenarios and the best possible outcomes and write them both down. Use the quotes inside this journal as a jumping-off point for observations and explorations if you can't think of how to start. Write whatever comes, and don't criticize it; journaling is a means of self-reflection, not a structured composition. In other words, spew.

Finally, determine a home for your journal where you can reference it when the fears take hold. Keep it by your bed, since the worst, and often the most ridiculous, worries come in the middle of the night. Or keep it in the kitchen so that when you're panicking you grab it before the ice cream or the Mallomars.

There will always be days when you can take the advice that Charlotte the spider gives to Wilbur the pig in E. B. White's *Charlotte's Web*: "Never hurry and never worry." But on most days, you'll probably worry anyway. If you're going to freak out, do it right. Pull out this journal and write as much as you need. When you're done writing, throw on some headphones and dance like an idiot to Chic's disco-era hit "Le Freak." That'll cure anything.

If you want to make the right decision for the future, fear is not a very good consultant.

MARKUS DOHLE

WHY I'M SO FREAKING FREAKED OUT TODAY:

_____

_____

_____

_____

TODAY'S STRESS LEVEL:

The truth is that monsters are real, and ghosts are real, too. They live inside us, and sometimes they win.

STEPHEN KING

WHY I'M SO FREAKING FREAKED OUT TODAY:

_____

_____

_____

_____

_____

_____

_____

_____

_____

_____

_____

_____

_____

_____

_____

_____

_____

_____

_____

_____

_____

_____

_____

_____

_____

TODAY'S STRESS LEVEL:

There is nothing either good or bad, but thinking makes it so.

WILLIAM SHAKESPEARE

WHY I'M SO FREAKING FREAKED OUT TODAY:

_____

_____

_____

_____

_____

_____

_____

_____

_____

_____

_____

_____

_____

_____

_____

_____

_____

_____

_____

_____

_____

_____

_____

_____

_____

TODAY'S STRESS LEVEL:

He was alone with his thoughts. They were extremely unpleasant thoughts and he would rather have had a chaperon.

———

DOUGLAS ADAMS

WHY I'M SO FREAKING FREAKED OUT TODAY:

TODAY'S STRESS LEVEL:

"Blorft" is an adjective I just made up that means "Completely overwhelmed but proceeding as if everything is fine and reacting to the stress with the torpor of a possum."

TINA FEY

WHY I'M SO FREAKING FREAKED OUT TODAY:

_____

_____

_____

_____

_____

_____

_____

_____

_____

_____

_____

_____

_____

_____

_____

_____

_____

_____

_____

_____

_____

_____

_____

_____

_____

TODAY'S STRESS LEVEL:

There's nothing wrong with fear; the only mistake is to let it stop you in your tracks.

TWYLA THARP

WHY I'M SO FREAKING FREAKED OUT TODAY:

_____

_____

_____

_____

_____

_____

_____

_____

_____

_____

_____

_____

_____

_____

_____

_____

_____

_____

_____

_____

_____

_____

_____

_____

_____

_____

TODAY'S STRESS LEVEL:

In a dark time, the eye begins to see.

THEODORE ROETHKE

WHY I'M SO FREAKING FREAKED OUT TODAY:

_____

_____

_____

_____

_____

_____

_____

_____

_____

_____

_____

_____

_____

_____

_____

_____

_____

_____

_____

_____

_____

_____

_____

_____

_____

_____

_____

TODAY'S STRESS LEVEL:

A jewel's just a rock put under enormous heat and pressure. Extraordinary things are always hiding in places people never think to look.

JODI PICOULT

WHY I'M SO FREAKING FREAKED OUT TODAY:

_____

_____

_____

_____

_____

_____

_____

_____

_____

_____

_____

_____

_____

_____

_____

_____

_____

_____

_____

_____

_____

_____

_____

_____

_____

_____

TODAY'S STRESS LEVEL:

My ordinary state of mind is very much
like the waiting room at the DMV.

LEONARD COHEN

DATE

WHY I'M SO FREAKING FREAKED OUT TODAY:

_____

_____

_____

_____

_____

_____

_____

_____

_____

_____

_____

_____

_____

_____

_____

_____

_____

_____

_____

_____

_____

_____

_____

_____

_____

_____

_____

TODAY'S STRESS LEVEL:

I feel like I could
throw off sparks,
or break a window—
maybe rearrange
all the furniture.

RAYMOND CARVER

WHY I'M SO FREAKING FREAKED OUT TODAY:

_____

_____

_____

_____

_____

_____

_____

_____

_____

_____

_____

_____

_____

_____

_____

_____

_____

_____

_____

_____

_____

_____

_____

_____

TODAY'S STRESS LEVEL:

We are in many many troubles for the moment, so many that grief loses its dignity and bursts out laughing.

ROBERT FROST

WHY I'M SO FREAKING FREAKED OUT TODAY:

_____

_____

_____

_____

_____

_____

_____

_____

_____

_____

_____

_____

_____

_____

_____

_____

_____

_____

_____

_____

_____

_____

TODAY'S STRESS LEVEL:

Life is difficult, and complicated and beyond anyone's total control, and the humility to know that will enable you to survive its vicissitudes.

J. K. ROWLING

WHY I'M SO FREAKING FREAKED OUT TODAY:

_____
_____
_____
_____
_____
_____
_____
_____
_____
_____
_____
_____
_____
_____
_____
_____
_____
_____
_____
_____
_____
_____
_____
_____

TODAY'S STRESS LEVEL:

And when things start to happen,
don't worry. Don't stew.
Just go right along.
You'll start happening too.

DR. SEUSS

WHY I'M SO FREAKING FREAKED OUT TODAY:

_____

_____

_____

_____

_____

_____

_____

_____

_____

_____

_____

_____

_____

_____

_____

_____

_____

_____

_____

_____

_____

_____

_____

_____

TODAY'S STRESS LEVEL:

Quite collected at cocktail parties,
meanwhile in my head
I'm undergoing open-heart surgery.

ANNE SEXTON

DATE

WHY I'M SO FREAKING FREAKED OUT TODAY:

TODAY'S STRESS LEVEL:

In the dark times

Will there also be
   singing?

Yes, there will also be
   singing

About the dark times.

BERTOLT BRECHT

WHY I'M SO FREAKING FREAKED OUT TODAY:

_____

_____

_____

_____

_____

_____

_____

_____

_____

_____

_____

_____

_____

_____

_____

_____

_____

_____

_____

_____

_____

_____

_____

_____

_____

TODAY'S STRESS LEVEL:

I found the third grade to be very stressful academically.

JONATHAN AMES

WHY I'M SO FREAKING FREAKED OUT TODAY:

_____

_____

_____

_____

_____

_____

_____

_____

_____

_____

_____

_____

_____

_____

_____

_____

_____

_____

_____

_____

_____

_____

_____

_____

TODAY'S STRESS LEVEL:

The ultimate measure of a man is not where he stands in moments of comfort and convenience, but where he stands at times of challenge and controversy.

MARTIN LUTHER KING, JR.

DATE		

WHY I'M SO FREAKING FREAKED OUT TODAY:

_____

_____

_____

_____

_____

_____

_____

_____

_____

_____

_____

_____

_____

_____

_____

_____

_____

_____

_____

_____

TODAY'S STRESS LEVEL:

I have woven a parachute out of everything broken.

WILLIAM STAFFORD

WHY I'M SO FREAKING FREAKED OUT TODAY:

_____

_____

_____

_____

_____

_____

_____

_____

_____

_____

_____

_____

_____

_____

_____

_____

_____

_____

_____

_____

_____

_____

_____

TODAY'S STRESS LEVEL:

This sounds so bleak when I say it, but we need some delusions to keep us going. And the people who successfully delude themselves seem happier than the people who can't.

WOODY ALLEN

WHY I'M SO FREAKING FREAKED OUT TODAY:

_____

_____

_____

_____

_____

_____

_____

_____

_____

_____

_____

_____

_____

_____

_____

_____

_____

_____

_____

_____

_____

_____

_____

_____

TODAY'S STRESS LEVEL:

Woe-is-me is not an attractive narrative.

MAUREEN DOWD

WHY I'M SO FREAKING FREAKED OUT TODAY:

_____

_____

_____

_____

_____

_____

_____

_____

_____

_____

_____

_____

_____

_____

_____

_____

_____

_____

_____

_____

_____

_____

_____

_____

_____

TODAY'S STRESS LEVEL:

In times of great stress and adversity, it's always best to keep busy, to plow your anger and your energy into something positive.

LEE IACOCCA

WHY I'M SO FREAKING FREAKED OUT TODAY:

_____

_____

_____

_____

_____

_____

_____

_____

_____

_____

_____

_____

_____

_____

_____

_____

_____

_____

_____

_____

_____

TODAY'S STRESS LEVEL:

What if you do fail, and get fairly rolled in the dirt once or twice? Up again, you shall never be so afraid of a tumble.

RALPH WALDO EMERSON

DATE		

WHY I'M SO FREAKING FREAKED OUT TODAY:

_____

_____

_____

_____

_____

_____

_____

_____

_____

_____

_____

_____

_____

_____

_____

_____

_____

_____

_____

_____

_____

_____

_____

_____

_____

TODAY'S STRESS LEVEL:

There must
be quite a few
things that
a hot bath
won't cure,
but I don't
know many
of them.

SYLVIA PLATH

WHY I'M SO FREAKING FREAKED OUT TODAY:

_____

_____

_____

_____

_____

_____

_____

_____

_____

_____

_____

_____

_____

_____

_____

_____

_____

_____

_____

_____

_____

_____

_____

_____

_____

_____

_____

_____

TODAY'S STRESS LEVEL:

Every time you are tempted to react
in the same old way, ask if you want
to be a prisoner of the past or a pioneer
of the future.

DEEPAK CHOPRA

DATE		

WHY I'M SO FREAKING FREAKED OUT TODAY:

_____

_____

_____

_____

_____

_____

_____

_____

_____

_____

_____

_____

_____

_____

_____

_____

_____

_____

_____

_____

_____

_____

_____

_____

TODAY'S STRESS LEVEL:

Panic—a deep abiding, free-floating anxiety, often without any reason or logical basis.

NELSON DEMILLE

DATE

WHY I'M SO FREAKING FREAKED OUT TODAY:

_____
_____
_____
_____
_____
_____
_____
_____
_____
_____
_____
_____
_____
_____
_____
_____
_____
_____
_____
_____
_____
_____
_____
_____

TODAY'S STRESS LEVEL:

I fail and I go on. Failure is a beginning, failure is the springboard of hope.

CARLA NEEDLEMAN

	DATE	

WHY I'M SO FREAKING FREAKED OUT TODAY:

_____

_____

_____

_____

_____

_____

_____

_____

_____

_____

_____

_____

_____

_____

_____

_____

_____

_____

_____

_____

_____

_____

TODAY'S STRESS LEVEL:

To allow oneself to be carried away
by a multitude of conflicting concerns,
to surrender to too many demands,
to commit oneself to too many projects,
to want to help everyone in everything
is to succumb to violence.

THOMAS MERTON

WHY I'M SO FREAKING FREAKED OUT TODAY:

TODAY'S STRESS LEVEL:

I've got to start listening to those quiet, nagging doubts.

BILL WATTERSON

DATE		

WHY I'M SO FREAKING FREAKED OUT TODAY:

_____

_____

_____

_____

_____

_____

_____

_____

_____

_____

_____

_____

_____

_____

_____

_____

_____

_____

_____

_____

_____

_____

_____

_____

_____

TODAY'S STRESS LEVEL:

Our doubt is our passion and
our passion is our task. The rest
is the madness of art.

HENRY JAMES

WHY I'M SO FREAKING FREAKED OUT TODAY:

_____
_____
_____
_____
_____
_____
_____
_____
_____
_____
_____
_____
_____
_____
_____
_____
_____
_____
_____
_____
_____
_____
_____
_____

TODAY'S STRESS LEVEL:

To think you can change your life by changing its outward conditions is just like thinking, as I did as a boy, that by sitting on a stick and taking hold of it at both ends I could lift myself up.

LEO TOLSTOY

WHY I'M SO FREAKING FREAKED OUT TODAY:

_____

_____

_____

_____

_____

_____

_____

_____

_____

_____

_____

_____

_____

_____

_____

_____

_____

_____

_____

_____

_____

_____

_____

TODAY'S STRESS LEVEL:

You may not control all the events that happen to you, but you can decide not to be reduced by them.

MAYA ANGELOU

WHY I'M SO FREAKING FREAKED OUT TODAY:

_____
_____
_____
_____
_____
_____
_____
_____
_____
_____
_____
_____
_____
_____
_____
_____
_____
_____
_____
_____
_____
_____
_____
_____

TODAY'S STRESS LEVEL:

I'd love to tell you I had some deep revelation on my way down, that I came to terms with my own mortality, laughed in the face of death, et cetera.

The truth? My only thought was: Aaaaggghhhhh!

RICK RIORDAN

WHY I'M SO FREAKING FREAKED OUT TODAY:

_____

_____

_____

_____

_____

_____

_____

_____

_____

_____

_____

_____

_____

_____

_____

_____

_____

_____

_____

_____

_____

_____

_____

_____

_____

TODAY'S STRESS LEVEL:

It is a common
experience that a
problem difficult at
night is resolved in
the morning after the
committee of sleep has
worked on it.

JOHN STEINBECK

WHY I'M SO FREAKING FREAKED OUT TODAY:

_____

_____

_____

_____

_____

_____

_____

_____

_____

_____

_____

_____

_____

_____

_____

_____

_____

_____

_____

_____

_____

_____

_____

TODAY'S STRESS LEVEL:

Sometimes the most intelligent thing is not to do anything, certainly nothing loaded with the imbecility of emotionality.

WILLIAM SAROYAN

WHY I'M SO FREAKING FREAKED OUT TODAY:

_____

_____

_____

_____

_____

_____

_____

_____

_____

_____

_____

_____

_____

_____

_____

_____

_____

_____

_____

_____

_____

_____

_____

_____

_____

_____

TODAY'S STRESS LEVEL:

My mind turned by anxiety, or other cause, from its scrutiny of blank paper, is like a lost child—wandering the house, sitting on the bottom step to cry.

VIRGINIA WOOLF

WHY I'M SO FREAKING FREAKED OUT TODAY:

_____

_____

_____

_____

_____

_____

_____

_____

_____

_____

_____

_____

_____

_____

_____

_____

_____

_____

_____

_____

_____

_____

_____

_____

_____

TODAY'S STRESS LEVEL:

I write to explore all the things I'm afraid of.

JOSS WHEDON

WHY I'M SO FREAKING FREAKED OUT TODAY:

_____

_____

_____

_____

_____

_____

_____

_____

_____

_____

_____

_____

_____

_____

_____

_____

_____

_____

_____

_____

_____

_____

_____

_____

TODAY'S STRESS LEVEL:

Outer order contributes to inner calm.

GRETCHEN RUBIN

WHY I'M SO FREAKING FREAKED OUT TODAY:

_____

_____

_____

_____

_____

_____

_____

_____

_____

_____

_____

_____

_____

_____

_____

_____

_____

_____

_____

_____

_____

_____

_____

_____

TODAY'S STRESS LEVEL:

You can tell a lot from a person's nails. When a life starts to unravel, they're among the first to go.

IAN MCEWAN

WHY I'M SO FREAKING FREAKED OUT TODAY:

_____

_____

_____

_____

_____

_____

_____

_____

_____

_____

_____

_____

_____

_____

_____

_____

_____

_____

_____

_____

_____

_____

_____

_____

_____

TODAY'S STRESS LEVEL:

Fear is the mind-killer.

FRANK HERBERT

WHY I'M SO FREAKING FREAKED OUT TODAY:

_____

_____

_____

_____

_____

_____

_____

_____

_____

_____

_____

_____

_____

_____

_____

_____

_____

_____

_____

_____

_____

_____

_____

_____

_____

_____

TODAY'S STRESS LEVEL:

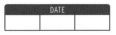

But we also know that only those who dare to fail greatly, can ever achieve greatly.

ROBERT F. KENNEDY

WHY I'M SO FREAKING FREAKED OUT TODAY:

_____

_____

_____

_____

_____

_____

_____

_____

_____

_____

_____

_____

_____

_____

_____

_____

_____

_____

_____

_____

_____

_____

_____

_____

TODAY'S STRESS LEVEL:

Unease, anxiety, tension, stress, worry—all forms of fear—are caused by too much future, and not enough presence.

———

ECKHART TOLLE

WHY I'M SO FREAKING FREAKED OUT TODAY:

_____

_____

_____

_____

_____

_____

_____

_____

_____

_____

_____

_____

_____

_____

_____

_____

_____

_____

_____

_____

_____

TODAY'S STRESS LEVEL:

Anxiety and Ennui are the Scylla and Charybdis on which the bark of human happiness is most commonly wrecked.

WILLIAM EDWARD HARTPOLE LECKY

DATE

WHY I'M SO FREAKING FREAKED OUT TODAY:

_____
_____
_____
_____
_____
_____
_____
_____
_____
_____
_____
_____
_____
_____
_____
_____
_____
_____
_____
_____
_____
_____
_____

TODAY'S STRESS LEVEL:

Now
That
All your worry
Has proved such an
Unlucrative
Business,
Why
Not
Find a better
Job.

—
HAFIZ

DATE

WHY I'M SO FREAKING FREAKED OUT TODAY:

_____

_____

_____

_____

_____

_____

_____

_____

_____

_____

_____

_____

_____

_____

_____

_____

_____

_____

_____

_____

_____

_____

TODAY'S STRESS LEVEL:

Let everything happen to you:
beauty and terror.
Only press on: no feeling is final.

———————————

RAINER MARIA RILKE

WHY I'M SO FREAKING FREAKED OUT TODAY:

_____

_____

_____

_____

_____

_____

_____

_____

_____

_____

_____

_____

_____

_____

_____

_____

_____

_____

_____

_____

_____

_____

_____

_____

TODAY'S STRESS LEVEL:

You know what a thorough sufferer I can be. I not only hit bottom, I walk for miles and miles on it.

———————

SAUL BELLOW

WHY I'M SO FREAKING FREAKED OUT TODAY:

_____
_____
_____
_____
_____
_____
_____
_____
_____
_____
_____
_____
_____
_____
_____
_____
_____
_____
_____
_____
_____
_____
_____

TODAY'S STRESS LEVEL:

I really don't know
what to do when my life
is not chaotic.

CARRIE BROWNSTEIN

WHY I'M SO FREAKING FREAKED OUT TODAY:

_____

_____

_____

_____

_____

_____

_____

_____

_____

_____

_____

_____

_____

_____

_____

_____

_____

_____

_____

_____

_____

_____

_____

_____

TODAY'S STRESS LEVEL:

We are frazzled and unruly, you and me. We are desperate and wistful and restless and funny and frayed at the edges.

HEATHER HAVRILESKY

WHY I'M SO FREAKING FREAKED OUT TODAY:

_____

_____

_____

_____

_____

_____

_____

_____

_____

_____

_____

_____

_____

_____

_____

_____

_____

_____

_____

_____

_____

_____

_____

_____

_____

TODAY'S STRESS LEVEL:

Let the peace of this day be here tomorrow when I wake up.

THOMAS PYNCHON

WHY I'M SO FREAKING FREAKED OUT TODAY:

_____

_____

_____

_____

_____

_____

_____

_____

_____

_____

_____

_____

_____

_____

_____

_____

_____

_____

_____

_____

_____

_____

TODAY'S STRESS LEVEL:

We live
only a few
conscious
decades,
and we fret
ourselves
enough
for several
lifetimes.

CHRISTOPHER HITCHENS

DATE

WHY I'M SO FREAKING FREAKED OUT TODAY:

TODAY'S STRESS LEVEL:

Fear is contagious. You can catch it. Sometimes all it takes is for someone to say that they're scared for the fear to become real.

NEIL GAIMAN

DATE		

WHY I'M SO FREAKING FREAKED OUT TODAY:

_____

_____

_____

_____

_____

_____

_____

_____

_____

_____

_____

_____

_____

_____

_____

_____

_____

_____

_____

_____

_____

_____

_____

_____

TODAY'S STRESS LEVEL:

It's not time to worry yet.

HARPER LEE

WHY I'M SO FREAKING FREAKED OUT TODAY:

_____

_____

_____

_____

_____

_____

_____

_____

_____

_____

_____

_____

_____

_____

_____

_____

_____

_____

_____

_____

_____

_____

_____

_____

TODAY'S STRESS LEVEL:

I am often 15 minutes late because of my inexplicable anxiety about being 2 minutes early.

B. J. NOVAK

WHY I'M SO FREAKING FREAKED OUT TODAY:

_____

_____

_____

_____

_____

_____

_____

_____

_____

_____

_____

_____

_____

_____

_____

_____

_____

_____

_____

_____

_____

_____

_____

_____

_____

TODAY'S STRESS LEVEL:

But we wouldn't do much if we didn't do things that nobody ever heard of before.

LAURA INGALLS WILDER

WHY I'M SO FREAKING FREAKED OUT TODAY:

_____

_____

_____

_____

_____

_____

_____

_____

_____

_____

_____

_____

_____

_____

_____

_____

_____

_____

_____

_____

_____

_____

TODAY'S STRESS LEVEL:

There's a plague inside of me /
Eating at my disposition /
Nothing's left

———

GREEN DAY

WHY I'M SO FREAKING FREAKED OUT TODAY:

_____

_____

_____

_____

_____

_____

_____

_____

_____

_____

_____

_____

_____

_____

_____

_____

_____

_____

_____

_____

_____

_____

_____

TODAY'S STRESS LEVEL:

The social barriers in life are so intense and horrific that every encounter is just fraught with so many problems and dread. Every situation is a potential nightmare.

LARRY DAVID

WHY I'M SO FREAKING FREAKED OUT TODAY:

_____

_____

_____

_____

_____

_____

_____

_____

_____

_____

_____

_____

_____

_____

_____

_____

_____

_____

_____

_____

_____

_____

_____

_____

TODAY'S STRESS LEVEL:

Disaster is virtue's opportunity.

SENECA

WHY I'M SO FREAKING FREAKED OUT TODAY:

_____
_____
_____
_____
_____
_____
_____
_____
_____
_____
_____
_____
_____
_____
_____
_____
_____
_____
_____
_____
_____
_____
_____
_____

TODAY'S STRESS LEVEL:

The disturbers of happiness, in this world, are our desires, our griefs, and our fears.

SAMUEL JOHNSON

WHY I'M SO FREAKING FREAKED OUT TODAY:

_____

_____

_____

_____

_____

_____

_____

_____

_____

_____

_____

_____

_____

_____

_____

_____

_____

_____

_____

_____

_____

_____

_____

_____

_____

TODAY'S STRESS LEVEL:

Drag your thoughts away from your troubles—
by the ears, by the heels, or any other way, so
you manage it.

MARK TWAIN

WHY I'M SO FREAKING FREAKED OUT TODAY:

_____

_____

_____

_____

_____

_____

_____

_____

_____

_____

_____

_____

_____

_____

_____

_____

_____

_____

_____

_____

_____

_____

_____

_____

TODAY'S STRESS LEVEL:

Failure after long perseverance is much grander than never to have a striving good enough to be called a failure.

GEORGE ELIOT

WHY I'M SO FREAKING FREAKED OUT TODAY:

_____
_____
_____
_____
_____
_____
_____
_____
_____
_____
_____
_____
_____
_____
_____
_____
_____
_____
_____
_____
_____
_____
_____
_____
_____

TODAY'S STRESS LEVEL:

When we are angry or frightened it is not by our choice; but our virtues are expressions of our choice, or at any rate imply choice.

ARISTOTLE

DATE		

WHY I'M SO FREAKING FREAKED OUT TODAY:

_____

_____

_____

_____

_____

_____

_____

_____

_____

_____

_____

_____

_____

_____

_____

_____

_____

_____

_____

_____

_____

_____

_____

_____

_____

TODAY'S STRESS LEVEL:

Ever been in a spelling bee as a kid?
That snowy second after the announcement
of the word as you sift your brain to see
if you can spell it? It was like that, the
blank panic.

GILLIAN FLYNN

DATE		

WHY I'M SO FREAKING FREAKED OUT TODAY:

_____

_____

_____

_____

_____

_____

_____

_____

_____

_____

_____

_____

_____

_____

_____

_____

_____

_____

_____

_____

_____

_____

TODAY'S STRESS LEVEL:

Anxiety is love's greatest killer, because it is like the stranglehold of the drowning.

ANAÏS NIN

WHY I'M SO FREAKING FREAKED OUT TODAY:

_____

_____

_____

_____

_____

_____

_____

_____

_____

_____

_____

_____

_____

_____

_____

_____

_____

_____

_____

_____

_____

_____

_____

_____

TODAY'S STRESS LEVEL:

Scary, isn't it? But what wonderful thing didn't start out scary?

ISAAC MARION

DATE

WHY I'M SO FREAKING FREAKED OUT TODAY:

_____

_____

_____

_____

_____

_____

_____

_____

_____

_____

_____

_____

_____

_____

_____

_____

_____

_____

_____

_____

_____

TODAY'S STRESS LEVEL:

The world breaks everyone and afterward many are strong at the broken places.

ERNEST HEMINGWAY

WHY I'M SO FREAKING FREAKED OUT TODAY:

_____

_____

_____

_____

_____

_____

_____

_____

_____

_____

_____

_____

_____

_____

_____

_____

_____

_____

_____

_____

_____

_____

_____

TODAY'S STRESS LEVEL:

Each of us has his own rhythm of suffering.

ROLAND BARTHES

WHY I'M SO FREAKING FREAKED OUT TODAY:

_____

_____

_____

_____

_____

_____

_____

_____

_____

_____

_____

_____

_____

_____

_____

_____

_____

_____

_____

_____

_____

_____

_____

TODAY'S STRESS LEVEL:

When it finally briefly happens, happiness can feel very worrying.

ALAIN DE BOTTON

WHY I'M SO FREAKING FREAKED OUT TODAY:

_____

_____

_____

_____

_____

_____

_____

_____

_____

_____

_____

_____

_____

_____

_____

_____

_____

_____

_____

_____

_____

_____

_____

_____

TODAY'S STRESS LEVEL:

Just breathing can be such a luxury sometimes.

WALTER KIRN

WHY I'M SO FREAKING FREAKED OUT TODAY:

_____

_____

_____

_____

_____

_____

_____

_____

_____

_____

_____

_____

_____

_____

_____

_____

_____

_____

_____

_____

_____

_____

_____

_____

TODAY'S STRESS LEVEL:

There is no such thing as inner peace.
There is only nervousness or death.

———————

FRAN LEBOWITZ

WHY I'M SO FREAKING FREAKED OUT TODAY:

TODAY'S STRESS LEVEL:

Think of your
head as an unsafe
neighborhood;
don't go there alone.

AUGUSTEN BURROUGHS

WHY I'M SO FREAKING FREAKED OUT TODAY:

_____

_____

_____

_____

_____

_____

_____

_____

_____

_____

_____

_____

_____

_____

_____

_____

_____

_____

_____

_____

_____

_____

_____

_____

_____

TODAY'S STRESS LEVEL:

I will show you fear in a handful of dust.

T. S. ELIOT

DATE		

WHY I'M SO FREAKING FREAKED OUT TODAY:

_____

_____

_____

_____

_____

_____

_____

_____

_____

_____

_____

_____

_____

_____

_____

_____

_____

_____

_____

_____

_____

_____

_____

_____

TODAY'S STRESS LEVEL:

Our real fears are the sounds of footsteps walking in the corridors of our minds, and the anxieties, the phantom floatings, they create.

TRUMAN CAPOTE

WHY I'M SO FREAKING FREAKED OUT TODAY:

_____

_____

_____

_____

_____

_____

_____

_____

_____

_____

_____

_____

_____

_____

_____

_____

_____

_____

_____

_____

_____

_____

_____

_____

_____

_____

TODAY'S STRESS LEVEL:

I have a new philosophy. I'm only going to dread one day at a time.

CHARLES M. SCHULZ

DATE

WHY I'M SO FREAKING FREAKED OUT TODAY:

_____

_____

_____

_____

_____

_____

_____

_____

_____

_____

_____

_____

_____

_____

_____

_____

_____

_____

_____

_____

_____

_____

_____

_____

TODAY'S STRESS LEVEL:

If you have good thoughts they will shine out of your face like sunbeams and you will always look lovely.

———————

ROALD DAHL

WHY I'M SO FREAKING FREAKED OUT TODAY:

_____

_____

_____

_____

_____

_____

_____

_____

_____

_____

_____

_____

_____

_____

_____

_____

_____

_____

_____

_____

_____

_____

_____

TODAY'S STRESS LEVEL:

To be fully alive, fully human, and completely awake is to be continually thrown out of the nest.

———

PEMA CHÖDRÖN

WHY I'M SO FREAKING FREAKED OUT TODAY:

_____
_____
_____
_____
_____
_____
_____
_____
_____
_____
_____
_____
_____
_____
_____
_____
_____
_____
_____
_____
_____
_____
_____
_____
_____
_____
_____
_____
_____

TODAY'S STRESS LEVEL:

I'm not afraid of storms, for I'm learning how to sail my ship.

LOUISA MAY ALCOTT

WHY I'M SO FREAKING FREAKED OUT TODAY:

_____

_____

_____

_____

_____

_____

_____

_____

_____

_____

_____

_____

_____

_____

_____

_____

_____

_____

_____

_____

_____

_____

_____

_____

_____

TODAY'S STRESS LEVEL:

There's no place like om.

———————

KNOCK KNOCK